# Cryptocur

A Step By Step Guide To Building Your Portfolio:
Cryptocurrency Investing Explained With Real-world
Examples And Strategies

*(A Presentation Revealing Digital Currency AndBlockchain
Technology)*

## Rupert Brandner

# TABLE OF CONTENT

# Trend Channel

We already saw how if you connect up the highs and the lows, you can create a wide bar with roughly parallel lines, as we did with Amazon. These 2 lines define the trend channel. I actually like trend channels a lot as a way to trade, but you do need practice in drawing them properly. Regarding trend channels, there are a few factors that are essential for you to be aware of:

When a channel continues over a longer period of time, the trend becomes more powerful. (Don't forget about that Amazon craze! (We're talking over a decade of it!)

When a big trading volume is paired with a trend channel, the resulting indicator is more dependable than when trade volume is low.

If the price manages to move outside of the channel, it will very certainly continue to go in the same general direction that it has been moving in recently.

If a stock is consistently trading within around two percent of the trend, this restricts the possible profit you may make from trading it. A tight channel does not provide you much opportunity for trading. On the other hand, you have a better chance of making higher gains if you trade in a broad channel, which occurs when the main trend of the stock is accompanied by some degree of volatility.

One of the rare situations when it is worthwhile to trade a stock that is not currently in an uptrend or a downturn is when you have a solid horizontal channel going all the way across the page instead of up and down. You may have a company that, for example, has a specific amount of dividend yield, which implies that income investors have a tendency to purchase whenever it comes down to the bottom of the range and sell once it goes to the top - you don't need to know the rationale, just trade the channel. Purchase at the lowest point in the channel, and then sell at the highest point.

Additionally, you may establish your stop-loss levels and profit expectations using channels, which is an extremely helpful tool. If you purchase at the bottom of the channel, your exit strategy should be to sell at the top of the channel; however, you should place a stop-loss order slightly below the bottom of the channel. In the event that you have it incorrect, this will save you from being taken aback by an unanticipated outbreak.

In passing, I should mention that you can occasionally observe from a channel how long it typically takes for the share price to go from the bottom of the channel to the top of the channel. You now have a decent notion of how long your transaction will continue, allowing you to time it in a way that maximizes your profit potential.

Bollinger bands are one example of a more complex kind of channel that relies on volatility rather than price indications. There are many other, more straightforward types of price channels. But for the time being, let's just focus on the pricing channel; that should provide you enough information to make sense of everything!

Now that you have some stock charts, look for price channels and see if you can identify any of them. Check to see how many times the price moved inside the channel, and then determine whether or not you would have earned a profit if you had traded the asset each time the price either hit or came extremely close to touching the bottom line.

# Gaining An Understanding Of Cryptocurrency

Is it feasible to get wealthy by investing in cryptocurrency?

Erik Fineman, then 11 years old, took $1,000 from his grandmother in 2012, when Bitcoin had a value of $12, and invested it in Bitcoin with the assistance of his brother. By the time 2013 came to a close, the price of a Bitcoin had risen to $1,200, and Eric had become very wealthy.

At the beginning of 2015, he was the owner of an education firm, which he subsequently put up for sale for a price of 300 Bitcoins.

At the age of 18, Fineman had already amassed a million dollars in wealth.

Fineman was just one of many early investors in cryptocurrency who capitalized on their astute business instincts to amass a fortune.

Since the beginning of cryptocurrency in 2009, when Bitcoin was initially brought to the market at a value of $0.08 for a single coin and was quickly followed by Litecoin, Dogecoin, Ethereum, and many more cryptocurrencies, the value of a single coin has increased exponentially.

The Explanation of Cryptocurrency

Other digital currencies were able to gain traction as a direct result of Bitcoin's ever-increasing popularity, despite the fact that its inventor, who goes by the alias Satoshi Nakamoto, remains a mystery. Bitcoin was the first cryptocurrency ever created, which paved the way for the widespread adoption of further cryptocurrencies. It also led to the recognition of cryptocurrencies as a means of exchange, a capital asset, and an investment opportunity because of the security that blockchain technology provides for the digital transfer of money from one currency owner to another.

The purpose of cryptocurrencies is to serve as a fiat alternative to the currencies that are currently in use across the world, many of which are susceptible to devaluation as a result of inflation or are at danger of being seized by the government.

Trading cryptocurrencies offers a plethora of opportunities to turn a profit, and there are trading methods that may assist you in organizing these profit-generating opportunities into a logical framework that can be adapted in order to consistently assess and improve the effectiveness of your cryptocurrency trading strategy.

When it comes to trading cryptocurrencies, the two most significant tools that you need to take into consideration are technical analysis and fundamental analysis.

Bitcoin's Ascent to Power and Fall from Grace

The price of Bitcoin started to go up in the autumn of 2017, and by October of that same year, it had broken over the $5,000 barrier. It then doubled in price in November, reaching $10,000 for a single coin, and has continued to increase ever since. When December rolled along, the cost was getting dangerously close to $20,000. Observers and detractors referred to it as a price bubble, comparing it to the Dutch tulip fever that occurred in the 17th century. However, only a few weeks later, the price of Bitcoin saw a precipitous drop, falling below $7,000 in April of 2018 and falling below $3,500 by November of the same year.

The price of bitcoin as well as its volume had a fresh uptick in 2019, reaching a peak of about $10,000 by the month of June.

Despite this, by the end of the year, the price of Bitcoin had fluctuated to approximately $7,000, and it is continuing its downward trend at this time. History has a way of repeating itself.

When the market fell in March of 2020, the price of Bitcoin dropped to around $5,000, which was much lower than its all-time high of just under $10,000. Since then, the value of bitcoin has been gradually climbing back up.

# The Role Of Money As A Means Of Control

A new function is added to money when it is centralized, and that purpose is control over the individuals who desire to utilize it. The centralized organization is in command and has the ability to prescribe to individuals what they can and cannot do with their own money. As a result, a great number of individuals have pondered the issue of whether or not it is conceivable to have a digital (nothing physically required) monetary system with all of the benefits associated with it, but without a central party to place one's faith in. A system like this would consist of:

Anyone and everyone is free to sign up and participate.

Absolutely free of any borders or regulations on financial transactions.

Easily accessed at any time.

one that has guidelines that are easy to understand and follow for everyone involved.

Totally untrustworthy, given that the only thing you could do was put your faith in the system.

Extremely tough to hack, since there was no one entity in control of all the money.

It is much more resistant to attack if it has the capability of multi-signing, which means that the signing keys may be stored in a variety of places throughout the globe. There is not a single "safe" that a person may break into (for example, to take gold), but rather several safes all at once.

Let's compare this to the "gold standard type of money" even if in principle this seems like it may be incredibly beneficial:

Value-bearing asset? Problem, since if there is no one in control, there is nothing stopping anybody from producing fresh money, is there? The quantity of money is not subject to any regulation. As a result, this kind of digital money is not scarce and does not make a good investment. Therefore, in order for it to be a suitable place to store value, it must ensure that a one shown on a screen will always be a one and cannot be changed at the whim of a third party.

What is the mode of transmission? Because it is digital, it is superior to everything that is tangible.

What is the unit of account? Because it is digital, it is superior to everything that is tangible.

Where do we stand with trust? The ability to manage "money supply," "access," and "receiving and sending" are among the most significant challenges presented by a decentralized digital economy. Because of this, we rely on centralized authority for digital processing in the modern day; nevertheless, if there was a method for those issues to be resolved, we would have a monetary system that was quite close to being ideal. People have been attempting to find a solution to the issue of scarcity in decentralized digital systems, which are systems in which there is no one person who is in control, for a considerable amount of time. The year 2008 saw the introduction of a potentially game-changing solution to the so-called "double-spend problem," which will be the subject of the next chapter's discussion.

# When Day Trading, The Most Effective Strategy For Limiting Losses Is The Following:

The purpose of a request for a stop-loss order is to limit losses that are associated with a particular circumstance in a security. When holding long positions, a stop loss may be placed above a continuing high, and when holding short positions, a stop loss can be placed below an ongoing low. Unpredictability is another possible basis for it to exist. For instance, if the price of a stock is changing at a rate of roughly $0.05 per minute, you would want to set a stop loss order $0.15 away from your entry point in order to allow the price some room to fluctuate before it moves in the direction that you anticipated it would.

Describe in detail how you intend to keep the risks associated with the transactions under control. In the case of a triangular pattern, for instance, a stop loss may be positioned $0.02 below a continuing swing low in order to buy a breakout, or it can be positioned $0.02 below the example in order to buy. (The $0.02 is a matter of opinion; the fact is just presented for clarity.)

One strategy is to establish two different points for the stop loss:

A request for a physical stop-loss that is set at a certain value level that is appropriate for your degree of risk tolerance. In a nutshell, this is the maximum amount of money that you can continue to risk losing.

A psychological stop-loss that is determined by the point at which your entry criteria are being exploited. This indicates that if the trade takes an unexpected turn, you will exit your position as swiftly as possible.

No matter what method you decide to use to exit your trades, the criteria you use to do so must be clear enough to be able to be tested and repeated. In a similar vein, it is essential to determine the worst possible circumstance that you can manage to live through on a daily basis, both financially and mentally. When you reach this stage, you are entitled to the remaining portion of a day off as vacation.

Keep your boundaries and your layout in mind at all times. When everything is taken into account, tomorrow is just another (business) day.

After you have determined how you will join trades and where you will place a stop loss order, you will be able to determine whether or not the possible system is within your acceptable level of risk. In the event that the method presented you with an excessive quantity of risk, you will need to make some adjustments to the system in order to lower the risk.

Testing will begin after it has been determined whether or not the operation is within the acceptable level of risk. In order to find your entries, you will need to personally experience verified outlines while keeping track of whether or not your stop loss or goal would have been hit. Paper trade in this manner for a minimum of fifty to one hundred transactions, keeping careful note of whether or not the method was profitable and whether or not it lives up to your expectations. In the event that this is the case, you should proceed with trading the strategy using a demo account in an incremental manner. If you find that the strategy is profitable over a period of two months or more in a simulated environment, you need to proceed with day trading it using actual resources. In the case that the method does not provide the desired results, start the process again.

Last but not least, keep in mind that in the event that you trade on margin, which implies that you are acquiring your investment assets from a financier organization (and keep in mind that the margin prerequisites for day trading are considerable), you are surely increasingly defenseless against sudden changes in worth. Margin may increase the profits you make from trading, but it can also increase the losses you suffer if the deal goes against you. Therefore, the implementation of stop-loss orders is very necessary while day trading on margin.

# A Concluding Assessment

There is no one trading method that stands out above the others; rather, each approach caters to a different set of requirements. Day trading offers a greater opportunity for profit, at any rate in terms of the rate of return on smaller anticipated trading accounts. In a certain sense, swing traders have a far better chance of maintaining the rate of return on their investments even as their accounts grow in size.

The minimum required amounts of capital are subject to significant movement across the many different trading techniques and marketplaces. Day trading demands more time than swing trading does, but mastering any strategy requires a significant amount of practice to become consistent. Day training is the finest option for those who like doing active things. Swing trading is an option that requires less effort and less time commitment and is available to those who are seeking for it.

Increased Access to Banking and Financial Services in Least Developed Countries

According to Darlington (2014), one of the most important benefits of cryptocurrencies is that they make it easier for individuals to participate in the financial system even if they live in underdeveloped nations. Cryptocurrencies have the potential to speed up transactions while also lowering their associated fees. People will be able to use it like a bank account, which will enable them to carry out their regular business and put money away. (Honohan, 2008; Scott, 2016).

When compared to traditional methods of transferring money between bank accounts, such as the SWIFT procedure, transactions conducted using cryptocurrencies may be completed much more quickly and at a lower cost. According to Tapscott and

Tapscott(2016), it is possible to do this by removing the need for any third parties to be engaged in the transaction, which will both reduce associated costs and enhance the rate at which business may be conducted.

Bitcoin Cash (BCH)

Litecoin was one of the first cryptocurrencies to follow in the footsteps of Bitcoin. It was launched in 2011, and it is sometimes referred to as "silver to Bitcoin's gold."7 Charlie Lee, a graduate of MIT and a former engineer at Google, was the brains behind the design.

Litecoin is based on an open-source worldwide settlement network that is not maintained by any central authority. It employs "scrypt" as its proof of work, which is a cryptographic algorithm that can be decoded with the assistance of CPUs designed for consumer usage. Although there are many ways in which

Litecoin is comparable to Bitcoin, it differs from Bitcoin in that it generates blocks at a faster pace and provides a faster transaction verification time. A rising number of stores, in addition to designers, are beginning to accept Litecoin as a form of payment. Litecoin is the seventeenth biggest cryptocurrency on the market as of November 2021, with a demand capitalization of $14 billion and a token value of about $200. This places it in the seventeenth position among all cryptocurrencies.

Cardano is also known as Ada.

Cardano is a cryptocurrency that uses the "Ouroboros proof-of-stake" protocol, and it was developed by a team of cryptography professionals, engineers, and mathematicians using research-based design practices.

Charles Hoskinson, who was one of the five early founding partners of Ethereum, was one of the people who initiated the task. Following a number of disagreements with the course that

Ethereum was headed, he departed and eventually contributed to the development of Cardano.

Extensive testing and research that was evaluated by other people were used by the Cardano team in the creation of their blockchain. Over ninety publications on blockchain technology covering a wide range of subjects have been authored by the researchers behind the project.

## Contrast Currency With Money.

The terms "currency" and "money" are often used interchangeably in common parlance. When you look up these terms in a standard thesaurus, you will see that they are, in fact, classified as synonyms. However, their economic functions couldn't be more distinct from one another. If you are concerned with the long-term security of your money, it is imperative that you have a solid knowledge of the distinctions between these two terms.

Money used

Hard cash or cash in hand is what the majority of people understand when they hear the terms "currency" or "fiat currency." You may put the money in your wallet or bag, and it comes in several currencies such as dollars, pounds, pesos, and even yen. Paper and metal coins are both examples of currency that may be used in a country. Currency is the principal means of transaction in any given nation. In the past, precious metals like gold and silver were often used to create monetary units.

The transportation of these priceless items was quite challenging. It was proposed that a portable form of cash that served the same function as the current form of currency and was supported by these precious metals be developed. In the United States, for instance, there is a kind of money known as banknotes that is supported by precious metals like silver and gold.

At any point in time, these banknotes may be traded in for legal cash if the holder so chooses. The precious metals that are used for the purpose of supporting such notes are referred to as legal tender. The value of the United States silver certificates may be redeemed for its equivalent value in silver. In 1879, the United States decided to switch to using the gold standard. The legitimacy of the government that issued the currency was boosted by the use of precious metals as backing for the currency.

This supplied the essential level of confidence in order for these monetary systems to function properly. People were willing to use this monetary system because they were certain that their riches would be protected by the precious metals that backed it.

A Standard Made of Gold

In 1933, President Franklin D. Roosevelt and members of Congress began the process of removing the United States off the gold standard. Because of this, the people of the United States were unable to insist on being paid in gold for their money. The general people was also compelled to sell all of their gold coins, gold bullion, and gold certificates to the Federal Reserve at a predetermined price of $20.67 per ounce. This transaction had to take place before the gold standard was implemented.

After some time, this price was raised to $35 for each ounce of gold purchased. Because it held as well as controlled all of the gold, the federal government was in a position to successfully manage the money that was in circulation. Inflation was intentionally manufactured under the administration of Franklin D. Roosevelt in order to artificially boost the economy. The elimination of the gold standard, which was implemented with the intention of boosting public trust in the whole economic system, is the source of this situation's inherent irony.

In the year 1971, President Richard Nixon made the announcement that the United States would no longer convert dollars to gold at the price of $35 per ounce, and this led to the complete abandonment of the gold standard. As a result, people living in the United States were made familiar with the concept of fiat money, which is supported by nothing other than people's faith in the government.

Funds available

Money is sometimes referred to as commodity money, because it may take the form of almost any kind of item, from seashells to stone. The purchasing and selling of products and services, as well as the payment of debts, may all take place using this as a means of exchange. Gold and silver are valuable in and of themselves, in contrast to the valueless fiat money that is created and decreed by the government.

Because there are so few of them, precious metals fetch a high price. Precious metals have a limited supply, in contrast to the arbitrary nature of the printing of fiat money by governments. In contrast to currencies based on fiat, gold is unchangeable. These metals are eternal and cannot be produced or destroyed in any way. It is only possible to alter their form. This would continue on until infinity. Try applying the same idea to the paper money that you have in your wallet. It could work better. Because of the unique qualities that they possess, gold and silver have been appropriately used as money for a very long time.

The removal of currencies from this context has resulted in a disconnection between our faith and the value of those currencies, and this has made it possible for governments and financial entities to manipulate those currencies' values according to their whims. In contrast to gold and silver, the value of fiat currencies may increase and decrease with the economies of their respective countries, but the value of gold and silver will remain constant throughout time.

a state of instability.

The necessities of human existence have no direct bearing on the value of fiat currencies since they are not backed by anything tangible. They call for a negligible amount of economic input that is of a physical kind. As a result of the fact that central planners get to make all of these decisions, the amount of a fiat currency system is almost always off.

As a result, this leads to fluctuations in prices and an artificial slowdown in the economy's production and distribution of money. Moreover, this leads to instability in the market. Maintaining a position inside the fiat currency system makes it impossible to establish price stability.

Volatility in the economy

In most cases, a fiat currency has only a tenuous connection to the actual economic activity that takes place in the real world. As a consequence of this, they have a propensity to become uncoupled, and ultimately, after some amount of time, they will get free of their tethering.

There is no possibility that all of people responsible for fiat money can estimate the needed amount of fiat currency since an economy is the sum of millions of autonomous individual beings, and there is no conceivable way that this can happen. On the other hand, they are able to recognize the incorrect amount based on the results that it produces. A credit boom, depression, recession, or even economic collapse might be among these potential outcomes.

In actuality, the Great Depression began 16 years after the establishment of the Federal System in the United States. There are several factors that might contribute to economic instability. In most cases, the effects of economic instability are exacerbated by the use of fiat currency.

# Comparison BetweenCryptocurrencies And Centralized Currencies

The term "centralized currency" refers to monetary systems in which the production and distribution of money is controlled by a single institution. These institutions (like a central bank, for example) are responsible for issuing money and determining its value. In its conventional form, money is a homogeneous means to represent a nation or region's value of output. It also symbolizes the value of production in the old sense. On the international market, the value of a nation's currency will decrease in contrast to that of other currencies if that nation's Gross Domestic Product (GDP) decreases. The relationship between money and a nation's sovereignty may be somewhat complex. To provide one example, in today's Western world, the majority of nations use the dollar as a benchmark for determining the relative worth of their own currencies. To put it another way, if we were to go somewhere like the United Kingdom, we would have to convert our money into pounds before we could use it there.

Decentralized digital money takes the form of cryptocurrencies such as bitcoin. BTC is not produced by a central authority but is still in circulation. It is not attached to any particular region, and it does not exist anyplace in the actual world. Because the market itself adds value to the item, it may be used as a mechanism for trading things. When Bitcoin (BTC) was first conceived of, its creator, the shadowy collective or individual known only as Satoshi Nakamoto, had the goal of establishing a decentralized digital currency that was both free and accessible to people all over the world.

Transactions Made From Peer to Peer

The term "peer-to-peer" (P2P) may refer to more than one kind of financial transaction; it is not limited to Bitcoin or other cryptocurrencies. Apps such as Venmo and PayPal have been available to users for quite some time, and they make it easy for people to send and receive money from one another. They are far quicker than sending money via a bank, despite the fact that banks have also sped up their payment processes in recent years in order to stay up with the trends. But if we're talking about Bitcoin in particular, peer-to-peer transactions have the same foundation since they don't rely on a central authority or any other third party. When it comes to conventional currencies, PayPal transmits dollars that have been issued by the United States government as well as credit that has been supplied by companies such as Visa or Mastercard, amongst others. The decentralized and peer-to-peer nature of Bitcoin's transaction network enables users to directly trade Bitcoins with one another, eliminating the need for a trusted third party. This results in a reduction in time, which in turn makes the process of transferring money and credit easier.

The art of ciphering

To have a grasp on cryptocurrencies, it is necessary to first comprehend cryptography and the rationale behind why it forms the backbone of bitcoin.

The process of transforming plain, readable text into something that cannot be read, often known as a code, is known as cryptography. In the beginning, cryptography was just another word for encryption. Encrypting and decrypting, also known as ciphering and deciphering, are the processes that a cryptographer uses to transmit and receive secret communications. A cryptographer uses a specific method or key to interpret a coded message. The practice of cryptography has recently expanded into the fields of computer programming and mathematics. It serves several purposes, such as protecting secrecy and integrity (anyone who was not meant to get the text is unable to receive it or change it), authenticating a message and holding its senders responsible for the objectives of such communication, and maintaining confidentiality and integrity.

Cryptography may be broken down into three categories: symmetric-key cryptography, hash-key cryptography, and public-key cryptography. Bitcoin was the first cryptocurrency to employ public-key encryption, and other cryptocurrencies have since followed suit. A key is used in symmetric-key cryptography, which means that it is available to both the sender and the recipient. They encrypt and decode communications with the use of this key, which ensures that the contents are kept secret from any other parties. The Hask-Key encryption does not need a key in order to encrypt communications; rather, it relies on a mechanism that generates hash values. In the context of Satoshi Nakamoto's invention of public-key cryptography, there are two types of keys: the public key and the private key. Users are responsible for managing both a public key, which they put to use in the encryption process, and a private key, which is put to use in the decryption process. Because of this, cryptocurrencies are able to retain their transparency while still retaining their P2P transmission method. Everyone is able to see the total number of transactions, but not who got them or how they were distributed. You could also come across the terms "Asymmetric-Key cryptography" or "Elliptical Curve cryptography" while researching this idea.

# A Look At The Pros And Cons Of Using Cryptocurrency

The term "cryptocurrency" refers to either digital or virtual currency. It is exclusively available on digital platforms, and digital wallets are the only places where it may be held. When you have digital money, you cannot physically handle it in your hands like traditional currency. It cannot be touched, felt, or smelled in any way. Despite this, you may make purchases of products and services with it in exactly the same way as you would with ordinary physical money.

However, what are some of the benefits and drawbacks of using cryptocurrency? If you are aware of its downsides as well as its benefits, you will be more careful in the way that you conduct your business. Being aware of its benefits will motivate you to perform better at trading.

The Numerous Advantages of Using Cryptocurrency

To remain anonymous

The development of the Internet has made it easier to conceal one's identity online. You are able to maintain your privacy and anonymity while using cryptocurrencies. You have the ability to restrict the quantity of digital data that is shared. As a result, you will be able to take pleasure in increased safety. You are relieved to know that your identity will no longer be stolen.

Openness and honesty

Transactions involving cryptocurrencies are seen by all parties involved because they are recorded on the blockchain, which functions as an open ledger. This enables the data to be accessed by anybody at any time and in any location.

Accountability is increased when there is such openness.

## Obtainability of Access

You are free to investigate digital currencies whenever the mood strikes you. You are able to have fast access to your financial information so long as you have an electronic device that is capable of connecting to the Internet. You are able to make purchases and sales in real time.

## Defending Against Inflation

You may hedge your bets against the effects of inflation using Bitcoin, just as you would with precious metals. Using fiat cash prevents you from enjoying this benefit in any way. Cash in its physical form is intrinsically risky, whereas fiat currencies have a natural propensity to devalue over time.

Because of the fixed nature of their production, cryptocurrencies are limited in supply. This means that their value will always remain high. In point of fact, a significant number of political scientists and economists anticipate that some features of cryptocurrencies will eventually be adopted into fiat currencies.

The Downsides of Cryptocurrency in Today's World

To remain anonymous

Because of their anonymity, cryptocurrencies are susceptible to being abused by dishonest individuals. The deep web and underground markets are really two of the largest consumers of digital currency. Online transactions may be carried out by criminals located in a variety of locations throughout the globe.

The intricacy of it all

The concept of cryptocurrency is understood by a significant number of individuals. Despite this, there are still those people who struggle while attempting to use it. People with impairments and the elderly, for example, are more likely to be technologically inept.

People who are unfamiliar with blockchain technology and other aspects of decentralized financial systems may be reluctant to adopt cryptocurrencies out of worry that they would lose their money. After all, after your digital money has been spent, it is probable that it will be extremely difficult, if not impossible, to get it back.

Security Threats

Hacking and other forms of cyber theft are a risk with digital currencies just as they are with other types of technology. You need to be on guard at all times since there are many con artists, hackers, and other crooks operating in the world today.

You need to have an understanding of the safety concerns and the security procedures. Maintain the same level of care for your cryptocurrencies as you would for traditional money. Do not give up your personal information and financial details too easily to persons that you do not know very well.

In a similar vein, you need to exercise caution when it comes to your various technological equipment. Always make sure you are connected to the Internet over a secure connection, particularly while you are signing into your online wallets. Because public Wi-Fi is not known for having a high level of security, using it is not recommended.

In order to prevent yourself from becoming a victim of phishing, you should avoid using public computers and should also avoid clicking on links that seem suspicious. Downloading programs that are not produced by reputable developers should be avoided at all costs.

It is also not a good idea to keep passwords on a computer, particularly if the machine is used by many people at the same time. If you like playing at online casinos, you should avoid giving your money to businesses that make promises that appear impossible to fulfill.

Variations in the Market

Purchasing things, participating in online gaming, and making investments are just some of the many uses that can be found for cryptocurrencies. If you want to make investments with your digital currency, you should hold off on doing so until the market conditions are more favorable to your position. It is essential to do out study and keep abreast of the most recent industry developments. In such case, you run the risk of suffering significant losses on the digital market.

## The Meaning OfCryptocurrency In Today's World

At first look, cryptocurrencies such as bitcoin and ethereum are distinct from fiat currencies such as the dollar. People have the opinion that because cryptocurrencies are virtual currencies and do not have any backing from governments, land, or actual products, their value is somehow lower than that of fiat currencies.

I do not agree with the claim that crypto is, by nature, less value than fiat money. While I do agree that crypto is distinct from fiat currency, I do not believe that it is less valuable. Coins denominated in a cryptographic protocol are referred to as cryptocurrencies. In the case of bitcoin, there is a limited supply, just as there is a finite amount of natural resources. Estimates of the amount of gold, copper, and coal that can be mined range from the millions to the billions to the even the trillions of tons. There will never be more than around 21 million bitcoins in circulation, and mining them will get progressively more difficult over time. It is stated in the frequently asked questions section of the bitcoin website that "the last block that will generate coins will be block #6,929,999, which should be generated at or near the year 2140." The total amount of coins that are currently in circulation will thereafter not change and will continue to be 20,999,999.9769 BTC." Bitcoins are not virtual currencies; rather, they are a commodity that is actively traded in financial markets.

When I talk to those who work in finance and economics, they tell me that at their most fundamental level, all monetary systems are really different belief systems. Gold is not even close to being the rarest metal on earth, despite the fact that its physical properties make it an obvious option for a pre-digital civilisation to utilize as a medium of exchange. However, gold is one of the few precious metals that can be found. In reality, mining gold is probably a simpler process than mining the majority of cryptocurrencies. It's not because gold is scarce that people believe in its value. How do we get people to believe in cryptocurrency?

## Stories heard while sitting under the Merkle Tree

She gave the frame of her brand new prescription AR glasses a little squeeze as she got closer to the entrance of the club. As soon as she approached the entrance, it seemed to turn green, letting her know that it had detected that she was older than 21 years old. A message along with a welcoming voice asked for the five dollars that was required for the ADA cover fee. She showed approval by nodding her head. After a little period of time, the door opened, revealing that the transaction could now be completed. A narrative from beneath the Merkle tree will now begin, and it will be about living in a society where there is no trust and no central authority.

Secret code

Ralph C. Merkle is considered to be one of the pioneers in the field of public-key cryptography. This kind of encryption is responsible for making it possible to conduct safe financial and commercial transactions online. The work he did on the cryptographic hash function, as well as the safety and effectiveness of his namesake Merkle tree, is arguably more astounding than the fact that he invented something that ended up transforming the world. If you haven't figured it out by now, the word "crypto" in cryptocurrency comes from the cryptographic hash function and Merkle trees. This is true even if you haven't realized it yet. Merkle trees provide an element of "fun" to fungible and nonfungible assets, give each block on a blockchain its own identity, and guarantee that smart contracts cannot be outwitted.

A Global Structure Without a Center

We've barely scratched the surface here. Those who have built upon the foundation laid by Ralph Merkle are about to usher in a period of increased individuality, privacy, and personal control on a scale that has not been seen before... oh... ever.

The technology described in the first line could be interesting to dissect in more detail, but let's keep it for another time. Instead, let's focus on a wireless transaction that is trustless and decentralized. The prospective customer's device sends a token to the club's system as soon as it is within range of the entrance. The club's system uses the token to identify the customer. The token reveals just one piece of information about the prospective customer, namely that they are above the age of 21, but it provides no further details. This one data piece fulfills the requirements of the first condition of the smart contract that governs membership in the club. After then, an automated request to pay the cover price of five ADA is sent to the prospective customer. ADA is a token that operates on the Cardanoblockchain and functions as a kind of cryptocurrency. The door will be unlocked after the last need of the smart contract, which is for the club's cryptocurrency wallet to receive five ADA tokens, has been satisfied.

# How To Make A Living Mining Cryptocurrency

Mining cryptographic currencies is a lot like taking part in a digital gold rush. First, you will need to purchase some equipment for a few hundred dollars and turn a little profit before moving on to the next step. After then, you have to put in months of mining time until the required difficulty level kicks in.

There are script-based cryptocurrencies such as feathercoins, dogecoins, and litecions. For novices, these cryptocurrencies provide the greatest cost-benefit ratio. For instance, based on the current price of litecoins, an individual might make anywhere from fifty cents to ten dollars everyday by utilizing mining gear designed for consumers. Using the same mining gear to mine Dogecoin and Feathercoin will result in a profit that is marginally lower.

Does it make sense to mine for cryptocurrency?

Mining cryptocurrencies may be a very exciting pastime that can also provide some unique challenges. After it has been set up and running, it will offer you one or two bucks every day. Regular individuals may mine a variety of cryptocurrencies with relative ease, including feathercoins, dogecoins, and litecoins. And if you put $1,000 on hardware, you won't see a return on that money for around 18 to 24 months.

as a secondary source of income. In point of fact, mining cryptocurrency or digital money is a solid source of income for the vast majority of individuals. You won't be able to begin earning $50 a day or more unless you are willing to make an initial investment of $3000 to $5000 in hardware expenditures. If you do decide to try your hand at mining cryptocurrencies, I recommend doing it just as a hobby or for a very small amount of money. If you want to use it as a supplementary source of revenue, rather than mining bitcoin, you should get started collecting and selling it.

How the mining of bitcoin really takes place

The purpose of mining, in and of itself, is to achieve the following three goals:

•Mining is essentially a kind of computer accounting that takes place around the clock and is known as confirming transactions. Therefore, you should begin by offering the currency network with accounting services.

• You will be compensated for your accounting services on a bi-daily basis in the form of change made up of fractions of coins. • You will be expected to keep your own expenditures, such as those for hardware and power, to a minimum.

The following is a list of things you will need to get started mining cryptocurrency:

•A cryptocurrency storage device known as a "coin wallet," which is essentially a free personal database. This wallet, which requires a private key to access, logs all of the transactions that occur throughout the network and holds your winnings.

•A free mining software suite that consists of the stratum and cgminer programs.

• You will need to become a member of a bitcoin mining community that operates online. A mining community consists of a group of individuals who share computers in order to boost both their income stability and their profitability.

• You will need to become a member of a currency exchange that operates online. It is essential to have it in order to convert traditional currency into virtual coins and vice versa.

•A connection to the internet that is both quick and dependable. A speed of at least 2 megabits, and preferably faster than that.

•A hardware configuration that is kept in a cool location, such as in your basement or in an area that is air-conditioned.

•A desktop or laptop computer that was purpose-built for cryptocurrency mining. You can get started with the computer you already have, but once the miner is up and running, you won't be able to use it for anything else. Therefore, you will require a second computer that is devoted to the task. If you want to mine cryptocurrency, you shouldn't use a game console, a portable device, or a laptop since these kinds of equipment are not strong enough to generate revenue.

•The pricey problem: In order to mine cryptocurrencies, you need a specialized processing equipment known as a mining ASIC chip or an ATI graphics processing card (GPU). These devices are required. The price of a brand new

ASIC chip or GPU may range anywhere from $80 for a used one to $600 for a brand new one.

•A ceiling fan to blow fresh air over your mining rig in order to keep it cool. Mining produces a significant amount of heat, and maintaining a cool environment for your computer hardware is essential to your performance.

• Curiosity on a personal level: You have a lot more to learn about this subject. Mining cryptocurrencies requires regular education since the underlying technology is always evolving. Miners who are at the top of their game spend hours each week researching the most effective strategies to make adjustments and become better.

Why don't you mine bitcoins yourself?

If you had begun mining bitcoins earlier, for example in 2009, you may have made a significant amount of money from the endeavor. However, mining bitcoin is no longer open to individuals and only huge corporations may participate. Over the course of the last five years, the mathematical problem of locating bitcoins has grown to be a very complex one. Mining is no longer profitable for home base operators due to the current initial investment as well as the additional maintenance expenditures. Mining bitcoins is currently not profitable unless the miner is ready to invest tens of thousands of dollars on an air-conditioning system and other industrial machinery.

## Using The 10-Day Period To Trade Demand And Supply.

EXAMPLE OF A CHART REPRESENTING THE SUPPLY AND DEMAND ZONE USING THE BACKWARD COUNTING APPROACH 6.

HOW TO LAY OUT THE PLAN.

From what we can see, plotting the graph or chart involves going backwards in time 10 trading days (shown by the space between the blue vertical lines) after the market has closed. As soon as the market closes on a Friday night, all you need to do is count 10 days backwards with the help of the session break so you know how to count per day. After that, you need to draw out the supply and demand zones within the 10 days period and expect the market to come back to respect the zones just as you have seen on the entry area. This will allow you to make profitable trades. It's possible that you'll only count five days on occasion, but keeping track of data across ten days will always provide the most accurate results. Have you noticed how simple the relationship between supply and demand may be? Let's look at a few more instances for the supply and demand during the last 10 days.

You should also keep in mind that you may not always need to count 10 days every time since it's always stressful; if you can identify the supply and demand as I mentioned in examples 1 through 5, then you are ready to go!

However, you shouldn't be worried about it since I will explain everything to you that you need to know in order to comprehend supply and demand. To identify them, I prefer not to use the 10-day strategy; I think that's because I'm simply too lazy to count backward, hehe. I am only responsible for identifying them, retrieving the order blocks from the zones, and searching for fractal entrance points. After reading this e-book, you will be able to pick the method you want to use to determine your demand and supply, as well as the strategy that will be most effective for you.

You may verify the date to confirm which was February 11 as indicated on the chart, which indicates that the analysis has to be done on a Friday night. Never forget that the 10 days were counted backwards after a Friday market close in the example 6 that was shown earlier. You can confirm this by looking at the chart.

Same strategy, the main benefit of using this 10-day strategy is that it makes analysis more simpler; you don't need a multi-time frame study, although I personally find that these kind of analyses are quite helpful. But this is also pretty effective and straightforward, although counting backwards can be difficult for you, particularly if you aren't very skilled at counting on your fingers.

Because we have to utilize the data during the first 10 days of this strategy, the time frame we require for the analysis is just 1 HOUR. This is because we have to collect it inside the first 10 days. That is to say, it is not going to function on the volatility index or cryptocurrencies due to the fact that such assets do not shut on the weekends. We need assets that are able to close on the weekends so that we may do our study when the market is closed and sleepy.

There is no particular approach to designing the demand and supply zones; rather, they are drawn in accordance with the explanations given in the first five instances. Let's have a look at example 7 below to see how the price responded to the demand and supply zone over the last 10 days. The demand and supply that developed in between the period of ten days are dragged out, and you wait for a mitigation. Patience is a fairly crucial part of this game.

This is how the analysis should be done according to example 11 from earlier; because it is a Friday and the market is closed, we count backwards 10 trading days from where the market is now standing while just utilizing the 1H time frame. When the market reaches the supply zone, which is what we anticipate it will do, we will begin searching for entry points to make trades from. Because there have been liquidity grabs in the past, we won't bother looking at the support zone.

.

We can see that the demand zone is the only one that has been drawn by looking at example 13 from earlier since the supply zone and the resistance zone have not yet been established. Don't forget what I mentioned earlier about demand and supply movements being forceful institutional moves that generally break highs and lows in the market; as a result, the demand zone is highly real.

EXAMPLE OF A CHART Number 17.

Labeled the secret OB on the H1 time frame, looking plainly without the understanding of hidden order blocks, you would never realize that zone is a good place to sell off from unless it was pointed out to you. Let's check the m15 or m30 time period to see whether an OB is going to pop up, which is required to turn it into a legitimate concealed zone.

 Now that the secret order block has been verified, all of us just need to wait for mitigation and wait for our entrance requirements to display before becoming engaged in the delivery of the price. Even after reading this, there is no guarantee that you won't do a back test because of how useful this is.

There is no approach that is 100% effective. Because everything we know is stored in our brains and our brains execute the job, our psychology also plays a significant role while we are trading and makes up a significant portion of the overall plan. I usually urge individuals who want to be consistent to sit down and analyze, then take trades more than 200 times doing the same thing over and over again to know how effective it works for you. If you want to know how consistent you can be, you need to know how good your strategy is. After doing that, you are aware of the areas in which you need help as well as your weaknesses immediately.

I really hope you are having fun with it so far, and if you are, please take a moment right now to hit the "subscribe" button on my YouTube channel by clicking this link, and also make sure you follow me on Instagram by clicking this link.

EXAMPLE OF A CHART Number 17.

If you didn't have the knowledge of hidden order blocks, you would miss the BUY move and keep wondering and asking yourself why your order blocks don't get mitigated every time; the most of the time, this is the primary cause. From what we can see here as well, we have two order blocks. If you didn't have this information, you would miss the BUY move.

Beautiful movement instantly at mitigation; while others are still waiting for the retracement to the lower order block, you have already entered the market and began milking as soon as you had your entry. This is in contrast to others, who are still waiting for the retracement to the higher order block.

Doing it from time to time repetitively, which is why I called it "the rituals of viewing the market from a precise perspective," makes you view the market accurately, taking and sacrificing your time to get what it takes. When you are able to follow all of the explanations that I have made in this ebook, you should not have any problems with the identification of demand or supply or order blocks. After gaining this information and investing your time, it will be with you for the rest of your life.

# The Complete List OfCryptocurrencies

Since Bitcoin was first made available, the use of cryptocurrencies has seen a meteoric rise. Even if the exact number of active cryptocurrencies is subject to change and the value of individual cryptocurrencies is subject to extreme swings, the market value of all active cryptocurrencies as a whole is generally moving in an upward direction. There are hundreds of cryptocurrencies that are being traded at any one moment.

The cryptocurrencies that are going to be discussed in this article are characterized by widespread adoption, significant user activity, and a relatively substantial market capitalization (in most instances, higher than $10 million):

1. BTC (Bitcoin)

Bitcoin is the cryptocurrency that is used the most all across the globe, and it is often regarded as being the cryptocurrency that brought the movement into the mainstream. Its total market capitalization and the value of each individual unit consistently exceed (by a factor of ten or more) those of the next most popular cryptocurrency. Bitcoin is designed to have a maximum supply of 21 million coins at any one time.

There is a growing consensus that bitcoin can function as a valid medium of exchange. Although many well-known businesses now accept Bitcoin as payment, the majority of them still work with an exchange in order to get their funds converted from Bitcoin to U.S. dollars before they are released.

## 2. Litecoin (LTC)

Litecoin was first introduced in 2011, and it has the same fundamental structure as Bitcoin. The key differences are a higher programmed supply limit of 84 million units and a shorter target block chain formation time of two and a half minutes. Both of these differences are outlined in the following table. The algorithm for encrypting data is also somewhat modified from before. In terms of market capitalization, Litecoin is often regarded as the second- or third-most popular cryptocurrency.

3. Ripple Ripple was released in 2012, and it is known for its "continuous ledger" system, which dramatically sped up the time it took to confirm transactions and create blocks on the blockchain. There is no formal target time for Ripple, but the average is every few seconds. Ripple is also more easily converted than other cryptocurrencies, since it has an in-house currency exchange that can convert Ripple units into popular currencies such as the U.S. dollar, the yen, and the euro.

Critics, on the other hand, have pointed out that Ripple's network and code are more susceptible to manipulation by skilled hackers and may not provide the same level of anonymity safeguards as cryptocurrencies that are derived from Bitcoin.

4. Ethereum Initially released in 2015, Ethereum introduced a number of significant enhancements to the fundamental architecture of Bitcoin. In particular, it makes use of so-called "smart contracts," which mandate the completion of a certain transaction, require the parties involved not to back out of their agreement, and provide a mechanism for reimbursements in the event that one of the parties breaches the agreement. Although "smart contracts" are an essential step toward addressing the lack of chargebacks and refunds in cryptocurrency, it is not yet clear whether or not they will be sufficient to solve the issue entirely. This

is despite the fact that these contracts are a significant step.

## 5. Dogecoin (Doge)

A variant of Litecoin, Dogecoin is easily identifiable by its mascot, a ShibaInu. It was created by the same people that created Litecoin. It features a shorter block chain creation time (one minute) and a far bigger number of coins in circulation - the creator's target of 100 billion unit mined by July 2015 was accomplished, and there is a supply restriction of 5.2 billion unit mined per year afterwards, with no known supply limit. Additionally, there is no known supply limit. Dogecoin is notable for being an experiment in "inflationary cryptocurrency," and industry experts are keeping a careful eye on it to see how the long-term value trajectory of Dogecoin compares to that of other cryptocurrencies.

6. CoinyeCoinye was created in 2013 under the original moniker "Coinye Wet," and is distinguished by an undeniable resemblance to the hip-hop superstar Kanye Wet. Wet's legal team became aware of the existence of the currency early in 2014, just before to the debut of Coinye, and they promptly sent its creator a letter demanding that they stop making the currency.

In order to avoid legal action, the developers removed "West" from the title, altered the logo to a "half man, half fish hybrid" that resembled West (a sarcastic reference to a "South Park" episode that made fun of Wet's naive ego), and continued with the launching of Coinye as they had originally intended. A cult following emerged for the currency among those who are enthusiastic about cryptocurrencies as a result of the hype and ironic humor that surrounded its release. In spite of this, West's legal team went ahead and filed a lawsuit, which forced Coinye's creator to liquidate their assets and shut down the website.

Despite the fact that Coinye's peer-to-peer network is still operational and the platform is technically mine the currency, person-to-person transfers, and mining activities have all ground to a halt, bringing the value of Coinye to a position where it is essentially useless.

# Tips And Advice

The realm of virtual currencies is experiencing a phenomenal period of expansion right now. It has been claimed that some individuals are making a lot of money in a very short amount of time after jumping on board the cryptocurrency train. There are still some open seats on the train, despite the fact that it is beginning to get very full.

This is a fascinating new idea market, and there is a great deal of data to take in. Despite the fact that this idea seems to be straightforward, you are really working on some code and algorithms. If you want to become one of the affluent Engineers of this incredible endeavor, you should be aware that while it is possible to get wealthy, it does not happen quickly, it takes time and a large amount of money to start, and it also requires understanding of all elements of this chance.

You should supply your subscribers with weekly and monthly market updates and share the specifics of your bitcoin portfolio with them. Maintain a vigilant watch on the latest news about cryptographic currencies, look into a variety of initial coin offerings, and keep your backers informed of any new opportunities as they arise. Over the course of the previous years, we were able to amass a fortune in various kinds of cryptographic money, and a number of our backers have shared their experiences, including early retirement, as a result of being involved with various types of digital money at an earlier stage.

While the first digital currency was established in 2009 for roughly $2, it has made quite a few individuals extremely rich in less than ten years. The sky is truly the limit for some of these digital currencies, and while the first digital currency was introduced in 2009, it cost approximately $2. According to recent data about the blockchain sector, "Ether" is now the second most valued cryptocurrency.

The first piece of advice I have is that as soon as you have your account set up, you should put some of your money into the "Ether" smart plan since that cryptocurrency is appreciating in value even as this book is being written. In 2015, one ether could be purchased for $11, but its price has already increased by at least 300% this year.

Ignore the Opinions of Biased Sources. This is the location where pump and dump schemes and several other forms of dishonest behavior are carried out step by step. There are a lot of people who post on websites that take crypto dealers into consideration who are fishing for fools by posting lies and gossipy tidbits and looking for financial professionals who will fall for it. Make every effort not to give them an advantage; instead, search for advice from reliable and objective sources, and make decisions on your contributions based on that advice.

Spend no more than you can afford to lose. Make every effort to avoid investing your life savings or the academic performance of your kid in electronic currency. It goes without saying that this is applicable to any endeavor; yet, it is important to reiterate that you should only invest an amount that you can reasonably afford to lose. Do you recall the age-old proverb that advises us to "Plan for the most exceedingly terrible, yet seek after the best?" This is related to that. If you plan your investments well, you'll be successful, but you should also be prepared for the possibility that you won't.

Establish Objectives That Can Be Met. We are forced to emphasize this point as much as it is feasible for us to: The use of digital currencies is not a quick way to amass wealth. We are going to presume that if you are wealthy enough, you are able to aim for the moon. However, for the rest of us, this piece of advice still stands: Establish a reasonable expectation of profit for your investment, whether it be 5%, 10%, 15%, or even more. In addition to this, be consistent! It is a young and incredibly strong market, and it has the potential to be disorderly; do not blow up, and stick to your long-term goals.

Do not freak out. Set aside some time to relax, investigate some of the most well-known companies in the industry, and focus on the current events taking place in the market. Do not make decisions on the spur of the moment.

Do not Rely Solely on Your Imagination. As was previously said, the elective money markets are notoriously unpredictable and are prone to moments of insanity. Do not provide your prediction of what the market is likely to do in the next period, regardless of how knowledgeable of a financial expert you may be. In point of fact, even the intelligent people who are excellent with their gut instincts will finish their task before acting on it. In order to behave in a similar way, it is helpful to follow patterns, read advice and news, and watch recordings.

Educate Yourself from Your Errors. Let's face facts: Any market may be compared to playing a game of chance with dice. No matter how knowledgeable you are in the field of finance, there will come a time when you will make a mistake that costs you money. Acquit the jargon, but when this occurs, pull yourself up by your bootstraps, wipe yourself off, and get back on the track. The most detrimental mistakes are the ones from which we do not learn anything useful.

Determine where you want to go. Learn how to read and interpret market diagrams, such as those provided by Bitcoin Wisdom, by familiarizing yourself with long-term market trends and practicing with those diagrams. Tracking your interests should definitely be done in a progressive manner; nevertheless, you should avoid making decisions based only on the changes you see occurring in your own self-awareness. It does not matter where your cash is donated from; purchasing and providing the relevant statistics information is of the utmost importance.

Honor thy cryptocurrency. Many of us get the impression that the world of high-end funds and Wall Street is dull and uninteresting, and that there is not a great lot of vitality to be found there. We have a deep-seated faith that this shouldn't be an issue with digital currency. In point of fact, you should not invest money under the notion that this is any one of the get-rich-quick programs; rather, you should do it because you totally believe the ideals and standards that underpin digital currency.

## Mindfulness Of One's Feelings

When I finally got a handle on this issue, I discovered that I had been poorly sized the trading positions I had been holding, but once I did, I was able to put an end to it. There is no hard-and-fast rule that dictates the size of your transaction, how aggressively you should scale into it, or even how large or tiny it should be. Each trader has to make a decision based on their own trading style, level of comfort with risk, and individual requirements. As you increase the amount of risk you are taking, you should monitor the emotional condition you are in so that you can attain that elusive "perfect balance."

If you acquire anything and very quickly begin to feel uneasy about it, you most likely have too much money invested in the play in question.

You are now in a situation that is so unsettling for you that it is difficult to tear your gaze away from the screen. Because you have invested more money than you can afford to lose and have no idea how to get out of this situation, every tick up or down causes you to break out in cold sweat.

Play only with the amount of money that you can comfortably afford to lose. This is one solution to the issue. In this manner, when you find yourself in challenging circumstances, it will be much simpler for you to maintain your composure and limit the damage to your bankroll.

"Be careful not to lose your cool. If your blood is boiling, then your business dealings will be freezing.

Taking a vacation from trading for a little while and allowing everything to calm down is yet another method for breaking this pattern. When we get extremely invested in something, we often find that we lose perspective and make errors that we would not have otherwise committed. You will be in a much better position to re-enter the battle with your wits about you after giving yourself some time to relax and gather your thoughts. Take a stroll and unload some of that mental and emotional burden.

Trading without paying attention to your surroundings is the same as gambling.

What we imagine and think about is likely to materialize into the world in some form or another. Keeping this in mind, you should see yourself performing well and being successful in the trade life you want to pursue. Make yourself your own best friend rather than your greatest opponent, and you'll put yourself in a better position to achieve your goals. Toxic and self-fulfilling thinking comes from negative thinking.

If you go into a transaction with the mindset that you are going to suffer a financial loss, then the odds are that you will. Take note of your state of mind as well as your degree of self-assurance. If you can't see yourself being successful, you shouldn't bother trying.

# The Process Of Developing Nft

Simply put, coming up with an NFT involves coming up with something digital. It might be anything, from digital art to photos, videos, animations, or even musical compositions; the possibilities are endless. You may have heard of instances like the one where a plain black backdrop was sold for hundreds of dollars, as well as many more cases that are quite similar to this one. This is the reason why this part is coupled with the section on the Reality Check of NFTs.

If you are a trained professional, you should have no trouble producing digital artwork of some kind. Even if you are not a trained expert, there are still a lot of different methods for you to make NFT.

There is nothing more satisfying than knowing that you, as a trained artist, are capable of producing work that is both extraordinary and original. Just keep in mind that you need to move quickly.

It is not about the actual labor, but rather about the marketing, hype, and trends in the industry. You don't have to start from scratch; rather, observe what's already successful and make an effort to develop something that is analogous to it.

Twitter and other social media platforms, in addition to the NFT market, provide the most useful information when searching for trends.

You may even utilize the website Canva. Be aware that using the work of another person might get you in legal hot water, so avoid doing so at all costs. You are free to create anything fundamental, so long as it follows the lines of the trends that are either now popular or likely to become popular in the near future.

The next option is to look into employing a freelance designer. This is by far the simplest way to acquire professional NFTs without doing any effort, and it's the easiest approach there is. Make it perfectly obvious to the freelancer from the very beginning that he will be used for NFT. This will help you prevent any potential disagreements in the future in the event that NFT gets popular. There are apparently some freelancers who are engaging in this practice. The site Fiverr is where you should go for anything like this. This link will take you straight to the page that lists all of the NFT freelancers.

When developing the NFT, keep in mind some of the fundamentals of human psychology. People make purchases based on their emotions, and the levels of those emotions are at extremely high levels in a bull market like this one. We are discussing feelings such as fear of missing out (FOMO).

The Operation of NFTs

In the prior chapter, I provided the groundwork to help you understand what Non-Fungible Tokens are by addressing their fungibility, the history that lies behind them, and their connection to cryptocurrencies. I did this so that you would have a better understanding of what Non-Fungible Tokens are. Learning the mechanics of how NFTs function can assist you in better comprehending the idea that underpins them.

Based on a Blockchain

Since the beginning of the internet, non-fungible digital assets have been there even before the development of non-fungible tokens (NFTs) and the subsequent acceptance of NFTs by the general public. In-game commodities such as in-game currency, domain names, event tickets, and user handles on social media sites like Twitter were examples of non-fungible digital assets. On the other hand, the standardization, liquidity, interoperability, and tradability of these non-fungible digital assets were not consistent across the board. Because of this, even if we have a large number of non-fungible digital assets, we have never really owned any of them in the way that the term "ownership" is generally used. For example, if you buy a skin for your character in Fortnite, you will really possess the corresponding in-game item. You will not be able to take the skin out of your Fortnite game and then sell it on a secondary market like eBay if you desire to do so. In a similar vein, you will not be able to use a skin that you bought for Fortnite in another game such as PlayerUnknown's Battlegrounds (PUBG). Therefore, the ownership of non-fungible digital assets is entirely dependent on the environment in which they are used. To put it another way, you only have ownership rights over certain digital assets within the context of the platform that provides them.

NFTs, on the other hand, are built on a specific blockchain, which means that this ownership issue has been resolved since their introduction. A synchronization layer may be provided by blockchains for digital assets, allowing users to get ownership and management permissions for such assets. This translates to the fact that with blockchains, you are able to fully own a blockchain-based digital asset, which gives you the flexibility to own and transfer such an asset for an unlimited period of time. Additionally, a number of one-of-a-kind features are encoded into blockchain-based digital assets. Because of these one-of-a-kind qualities, the connection that users and developers have with blockchain-based digital assets is altered.

There are a few characteristics that are inherent to blockchain-based NFTs, and it is these characteristics that distinguish blockchain-based digital assets different from the more conventional types of digital assets. These characteristics include, but are not limited to:

Conformity to Standards

As I was explaining before, the level of standardization that is applied to conventional digital assets varies not only according to the kind of digital asset but also according to the platform that it is released on. In light of this, we may deduce that none of the conventional digital assets has a consistent representation in the realm of digital technology. For example, the representation of an in-game item inside a game is going to be rather different from the representation of an event ticket within a ticketing system for events. However, since non-fungible tokens may be represented on blockchains, their developers have the ability to design standards that are universal, re-usable, and inheritable; these standards are applicable to all non-fungible tokens. Any NFT that is built on blockchain technology must comply with these requirements, which include the fundamental building blocks such as basic access control, ownership rights, and transfer rights.

If there is a requirement for certain extra standards to be added to certain

NFTs, such as specifications on how to display a certain NFT, then these new standards may simply be layered on top of the standards that are already in place. After layering a new set of standards, designers will be provided with a new set of what are called stateful rudimentary fundamentals.

compatibility of functions

Due to the standardized structure of blockchain-based NFTs, unlike conventional digital assets, Non-Fungible Tokens are capable of being readily moved across numerous ecosystems. This is in contrast to traditional digital assets. Therefore, as soon as a developer launches a new Non-Fungible Token project, the project is instantly visible inside various wallet providers, tradable on various markets, and may be shown within virtual worlds. This interoperability is made feasible due to the fact that blockchain standards offer an Application Programming Interface (API) that is unambiguous, consistent, reliable, and permissioned.

This API makes it simple to read and write data.

Trading ability

The interoperability of blockchain-based non-fungible tokens (NFTs) essentially makes it viable and straightforward to trade such NFTs across several markets. In addition, the interoperability aspect of blockchain-based NFTs makes it possible for free trade to take place on open markets. Users of digital assets based on blockchains, in contrast to users of conventional digital assets, have the ability to transfer goods out of the ecosystems in which they were first created and into new markets in which they may be sold. This makes it possible for users of blockchain-based digital assets to take use of extensive trade features, such as auctions similar to those hosted on eBay, bundling, bidding, and the option to sell in any currency, including stablecoins and application-specific currencies.

A State of Liquidity

Because NFTs may be traded instantly, it is reasonable to anticipate that there will be more liquidity. Therefore, creators of NFTs won't have to worry about liquidity issues as long as their products are underpinned by blockchain technology. Additionally, as the number of markets for non-fungible tokens (NFTs) continues to rise, these tokens are receiving increased exposure to a larger pool of prospective buyers as well as sellers.

# How The Technology Behind Blockchain Works

When individuals wanted to purchase or sell anything several hundred years ago, the only means of doing so was via the bartering of various goods. At that time, human evolution was still in its infancy.

For instance, if I had an apple but required firewood to cook supper, I would have to find someone who not only had firewood but was also in need of apples in order to arrange a trade with them.

Therefore, even if I located someone who had an abundance of firewood, it would not make a difference since the other party needed to be interested in purchasing my apples before the transaction could be finalized.

It is quite clear that the whole procedure was unreasonably stressful and was not suitable for use in all settings.

Therefore, a solution was devised to make things simpler, and the concept of fiat money was established.

Because of this, anybody who was in need of anything could now make a note offer to the other party, and even if the seller did not have any urgent requirements, they could keep the note until they were in a position to make a purchase, which made doing commerce a lot simpler.

On the other hand, this kind of money presented a number of significant obstacles.

People were required to pay taxes back then, yet there were also robbers throughout that time period.

People were putting themselves at danger when they kept their fiat cash at home since it exposed them to potential thieves. Additionally, the government was unable to readily monitor an individual's financial activity to ascertain whether or not that person was paying the appropriate amount of tax.

Therefore, the banking system was developed as a solution.

People now have a place to store their money until the time comes when they really need it, thanks to the establishment of banks.

But banking also brought with it a few drawbacks, such as a lack of privacy and a difficulty with trust.

In order to do business via the bank, you were required to provide a great deal of personal information about yourself, such as who you are, where you live, how much money you make, where you are from, how many children you have, and so on.

Trust was another issue that needed to be addressed. Even though banks are among the most heavily regulated financial organizations, it is not unheard of for banks to fail, and when this occurs, consumers often find that they have lost their money. In many undeveloped nations, this is a common occurrence.

In order to make use of a bank account, you were required to have faith that your money would be kept secure; seeing that there are no assurances, faith was the only option.

Paying individuals was also a bit of a challenge since if you needed to pay someone, you were required to either give them cash or a check. If you gave them a check, however, your personal information would be visible to the person receiving the check, and it was also difficult to pay people who lived in other countries.

As a result, a solution was developed: third party payment processors such as PayPal, Stripe, and Payoneer were created in order to assist in the maintenance of anonymity for customers who want to conduct private financial transactions.

In addition to this, it enabled individuals to engage in commercial activities on a global scale.

At this point, I want you to take note of something: the conventional monetary system that exists in the world today, as we know it, was developed as a solution to various problems; banks were invented to solve a problem; debit and credit cards were invented to solve a problem; and payment processors like PayPal and others were invented to solve a problem.

Since it is very unlikely that there will ever be a time when there are no problems in the world, and given that people have always been dedicated to finding answers to the many problems that threaten our existence and our mental well-being, blockchain technology was developed as a solution to a variety of issues.

# Exchanges For Cryptocurrencies Are Platforms That Allow Users To Trade Cryptocurrencies With One Another.

What exactly is meant by the term "cryptocurrency exchange"?

An online marketplace that allows users to purchase, sell, and trade cryptocurrencies for other cryptocurrencies as well as traditional fiat currencies like dollars and pounds is known as a cryptocurrency exchange. There are several distinct types of cryptocurrency exchanges, and each one caters to a certain demographic of customers based on the requirements of their individual transactions. There are advanced exchanges that provide traders the opportunity to engage in trading on a professional level, complete with access to a variety of sophisticated trading tools. Before you can open an account with any of them, the most of them will want you to provide proof of who you are. There are basic exchanges

104

that enable you to trade without the need to set up a trading account, and these exchanges are a good option for those who are just interested in making a one-time or occasional transaction.

Exchanges for cryptocurrencies may be broken down into the following categories:

Buying and selling platforms: These platforms bring together buyers and sellers and take a commission from each transaction. They handle the processing of orders and transactions, acting as an escrow service in the process, keeping both cryptocurrencies and traditional currency in their custody.

Direct trading platforms, sometimes known as peer-to-peer markets, are another name for these types of online marketplaces. Direct trading platforms, as opposed to trading platforms that serve as middlemen, enable buyers and sellers to engage in transactions directly with one another. The market price on direct trading platforms is never set in stone. The buyers and sellers negotiate their own rates of exchange.

Brokers and direct commercial exchanges are both types of websites that function in a manner that is similar to that of a foreign exchange broker. They make it possible for everyone to acquire cryptocurrencies in a straightforward manner at predetermined prices that are set by the exchange itself.

Considerations to Make Prior to Selecting a Cryptocurrency Trading Platform

Those who are interested in trading cryptocurrencies may choose from a number of different cryptocurrency exchanges that are now accessible. However, you shouldn't sign up for a trade just because it's the first one you've come across; that's not a good enough reason. Before you decide to participate in an exchange, you should think about the following aspects.

Reputation: The first thing you should do when thinking about using a certain exchange is to look through evaluations written by other individuals who have used the exchange, in addition to reading reviews written by respected websites inside the field. You may ask any queries you might have regarding an exchange by going to online groups and forums where cryptocurrency aficionados gather.

Transaction, deposit, and withdrawal fees are some of the costs that customers of cryptocurrency exchanges are required to pay. This is what ensures that they will continue to be successful. The fee arrangements of the various exchanges are distinct from one another. The vast majority of the most popular exchanges have a fee structure that is determined by the number of transactions conducted, which enables large traders to incur cheaper transaction costs. Make sure you have a complete understanding of the cost structure of an exchange before signing up with them. The vast majority of this information is readily available on the website of the exchange.

means of payment: Prior to signing up for an exchange, it is important to learn about the various means of payment that are offered and evaluate whether or not they are practical for you. Keep in mind that making a purchase with a credit card or PayPal will result in an additional fee, while making a purchase with a bank transfer might result in a lengthier wait until you get your Bitcoin.

Verification requirements: Before a user may deposit or withdraw money, the majority of cryptocurrency exchanges in the United States and the United Kingdom require the user to verify their identity. Other exchanges, on the other hand, let users to remain completely anonymous. Verification helps safeguard the exchange from being used for illegal activities like money laundering and frauds, despite the fact that it may appear to go against the ethos of cryptocurrencies.

Restrictions based on geography: Certain functionalities of certain exchanges may only be accessed from inside certain geographical areas or nations. Before you sign up for an exchange, you should check to see whether it provides complete assistance in your nation.

Rates of exchange: Various cryptocurrency exchanges provide varying prices for trading one cryptocurrency for another. It is in your best interest to do some research on the many exchanges available to determine which one gives the most favorable pricing for the cryptocurrency you want to trade in.

NMC stands for Namecoin.

It is impossible to find a cryptocurrency that is more intriguing and distinctive than Namecoin, despite the fact that it is still relatively obscure. In April of 2011, it was made available to the public as the first project to fork off of Bitcoin. Namecoin was designed with the intention of facilitating the creation of an alternative domain name service (DNS), which is the organization that is responsible for registering and maintaining a database of online domain names. ICANN, which stands for the Internet Corporation for Assigned Names and Numbers, has traditionally been in charge of maintaining this system's centralized supervision. Namecoin was developed with the goal of establishing a decentralized version of the Domain Name System (DNS) that would be immune to all forms of censorship and independent of ICANN's authority. To put it another way, the creation of Namecoin was motivated by the need to safeguard and, to some extent, regulate the right to communicate freely. Every single domain name that is registered using Namecoin is given the.bit extension at

110

the very end. This extension performs the same function that the more common.com and.net domain names do.

Bitcoin and Namecoin are both digital currencies, although Bitcoin is far more popular. For example, the total number of individual units available will be capped at 21 million. Miners may switch between Bitcoin and Namecoin depending on which one is more lucrative at any given time since the two cryptocurrencies are so close to one another that they actually use the same cryptographic algorithms.

Namecoin was created with the primary intention of building an alternative decentralized domain name system; however, it may also be used as a mechanism to set up blockchain support for things such as messaging and even voting. This was the original objective of creating Namecoin. The system was developed with flexibility in mind, and its primary objective is to make available as many opportunities as is practically possible in relation to the specific field in which Namecoin operates.

Visit namecoin.org to get more knowledge about Namecoin.

Mijin and NEM(XEM), respectively

NEM is an open-source cryptocurrency and blockchain platform that at one point had the intention of being a fork of NXT but ultimately ended up being developed from the ground up. However, its design is quite different from that of NXT, despite the fact that it provides many of the same features. A related innovation called Mijin is a private blockchain that was developed with the financial industry in mind from the ground up.

Proof of importance, sometimes known as PoI, is a novel approach to block verification that NEM implements. It is meant to require even less resources than the proof of stake algorithms that NXT use, which are already far less resource-intensive than the proof of work techniques that Bitcoin employs. PoI, much like NXT, is capable of running on almost any computer system, including a Raspberry Pi. Because of the way the algorithm is designed, it pushes users to make use of their tokens rather than just holding on to them in the hope that their value would rise. NEM has developed a mobile wallet that is solely devoted to promoting the use of its native coin, which is known as XEM, for day-to-day transactions.

NEM was developed to be a cryptocurrency that is both more secure and much quicker than Bitcoin. The integration of smart contracts, such as those offered by Ethereum, is another feature that developers are striving to bring to the NEM platform. Additionally, NEM is the first major cryptocurrency platform to allow support for the building of private blockchains.

Mijin is the solution to this problem. It is a private blockchain that promises to reduce the amount of time needed for transactions while also giving significant efficiencies gains. Along the same lines as Ripple, Mijin is one of the first cryptocurrency technologies to be examined by the mainstream financial sector. This shows that cryptocurrencies may one day be accepted as an equal method of trade to actual fiat money.

The website for Nem can be located at nem.io, while those interested in learning more about Mijin can go to mijin.io.

# What Is Bitcoin?

At this point, we should be able to have a more solid grasp of what Bitcoin is all about. Gaining more knowledge about Bitcoin offers you the assurance you need to start trading cryptocurrencies. The essence of Bitcoin, as well as its potential to have far-reaching and transformative consequences on society as a whole, is where the cryptocurrency's true value rests.

A Concise Overview of the History of Bitcoin

Bitcoin is the first cryptocurrency to have a lifespan of over seven years. It has achieved any kind of mainstream acceptance, but getting to this position required quite some time and effort. Before Bitcoin, there were a few other cryptocurrencies that had considerable notoriety. Earlier, in the part on the history of cryptocurrencies, we had a short discussion on David Chaum, a cryptographer who invented the idea of a currency that is backed by a secured computer program as opposed to a central bank. David Chaum is credited with developing this concept. His DigiCash had a short period of popularity, but it was ultimately unsuccessful in becoming the first cryptocurrency to be widely embraced. This e-gold that was established in the United States had the potential to become valuable in the cryptocurrencies that existed before Bitcoin. However, DigiCash was technologically distinct from Bitcoin since it had a centralized owner and its quantity was not set.

In August of 2008, Neal Kim, Vladimir Oksman, and Charles Bry submitted an application for a patent for a system including encryption. During the same month, the domain name Bitcoin was registered using the website anonymousspeech.com, which enabled users to create anonymous domain names.

A white paper titled "Bitcoin: A Peer-to-Peer Electronic Cash System" was released under the pseudonym Satoshi Nakamoto on October 31, 2008, and it was titled "Bitcoin: A Peer-to-Peer Electronic Cash System." In the study, many applications of the coin were shown. In addition to this, it included details on the blockchain technology and explained how the currency may be mined using just computer algorithms. Bitcoin was used in the first paper as an example of a deflationary currency and one for which governments would not be able to artificially raise the money supply, which would result in a decline in the value of a specific currency. In the white paper, Satoshi Nakamoto explains other problems with banks as trustworthy lenders, as well as how the blockchain's architecture for irreversible transactions might help lessen the danger of fraudulent merchants.

Beginning in January 2009, advocates began mining the currency, which resulted in the creation of the first blocks of Bitcoin. Nakamoto and some of the other early cryptographers began trading currencies with one another in exchange for services. The initial official exchange rate for the currency was determined to be one US dollar equal to 1,309.03 BTC and it was created in October of 2009. It was calculated based on the amount of power that would be required to mine one Bitcoin.

The first transaction in the real world didn't take place until May 2010, when Bitcoin enthusiast Laszlo Hanyecv bought two pizzas in Jacksonville, Florida, for the equivalent of 10,000 Bitcoins. Can you give me an estimate of how much 10,000 BTC is worth right now? That is more than forty million dollars.

The first significant hacking attack using Bitcoin took place in August of the same year. The malicious hacker was successful in revealing a flaw in the verification mechanism and produced around 184 billion Bitcoins as a result. Because of this, the value of Bitcoin, as a money, significantly decreased. The decline was only brief due to the fact that Bitcoin was able to achieve a market value of one million dollars for the very first time in November of 2010.

In January of 2011, Bitcoin was given mainstream publicity for the very first time. This coverage was of a respectable level. Silk Road, a website on the dark web that allows users to make and receive payments in bitcoin, was one of the driving forces for its creation. It was engaged in the business of trading illegal products such as narcotics and stolen credit cards. During its height, it is estimated that Silk Road was responsible for fifty percent of all Bitcoin transactions. Users on Silk Road were interested in the privacy that Bitcoin may provide.

In February of the same year, the price of a Bitcoin on the market reached $1 for the very first time. By the month of July, the value of the coin had increased to $31.

The year 2012 was mostly quiet, despite the fact that real-world adoption progressed when a hosting platform called WordPress began accepting Bitcoins in November. By March of 2013, the total market valuation of bitcoin had surpassed one billion dollars. In only one month, the cryptocurrency exchange known as Coinbase recorded more than one million dollars' worth of Bitcoin transactions.

The very first Bitcoin ATM was installed in Canada in July of 2013. China came into the picture when the activity on the Chinese market surpassed that of the US market. As of November 2013, the value of a single Bitcoin has hit $1,000.

The People's Bank of China issued a ruling against bitcoin in December 2013, stating that it was not a currency and forbidding financial institutions in China from accepting bitcoin as a form of payment. Mt. Gox, a cryptocurrencyexchange located in Japan, temporarily halted Bitcoin withdrawals owing to technical concerns in February of 2014. Within a matter of weeks, they submit their petition for bankruptcy amidst allegations of lax management and inadequate security procedures. Approximately 7% of the entire quantity of Bitcoin that was in circulation was lost in that occurrence, which equates to a loss of almost $740 million worth of Bitcoin. Because of this problem, the value of bitcoin fell by 36 percent in the span of only one month.

The United States Commodity Futures Trading Commission gave its blessing to TeraExchange LLC in June of the same year, making it the first time a US government entity has given the green light for a Bitcoin exchange to begin doing business. During this time period, technology company Dell began to accept Bitcoin (BTC) payments as a means of payment. At the time, it was the firm with the most experience in doing so. AirBaltic was the first worldwide airline to accept Bitcoin as a means of payment when it started doing so in 2013. Microsoft, one of the largest firms in the world, began taking bitcoin as a means of payment in December, making it the latest major company to do so.

During a fundraising round, Coinbase was awarded around $75 million, and the New York Stock Exchange participated as a junior investor. The cryptocurrency market is dominated today by Coinbase, which is widely regarded as one of the top trading platforms.

Additional scaling in the real world took occurred for Bitcoin. As of August 2015, more than 160,000 businesses were on board with the concept of taking Bitcoin as a form of payment. In December of the same year, reports surfaced about the possible identity of the person behind the cryptocurrency known as Satoshi Nakamoto. Wired magazine published an article stating that it was probable that Australian Craig Wright was the actual Nakamoto. This resulted in a number of incidents, all of which finally pointed to the conclusion that Wright was NOT Nakamoto.

The second "halving day" for Bitcoin occurred in July 2016, when the payout for mining one block was reduced to 12.5 Bitcoins from 25 Bitcoins. Previously, the reward had been 50 Bitcoins. This tactic was included in the initial conception of Bitcoin as a means of gradually reducing the amount of newly minted coins that were made accessible on the market. The subsequent halving took place in 2020, and the complete quantity that will be accessible on the market will not be reached until roughly 2140.

On exchanges, the value of a single Bitcoin is now $4,000.

# Where Exactly Do You Keep Your Bitcoins?

The following are a few different ways to "tore your Bitcoin," some of which may be safer than others.

Bitcoin wallets that are accessible online and can be used from any device with internet connection are referred to as online wallets.

Desktop Wallet An offline wallet has a number of advantages over an online wallet. Desktop wallets provide more storage space. Even though online wallets are simple to use from any location in the world, they are also more susceptible to being hacked than traditional wallets. Desktop wallets, on the other hand, may be accessed only via your own computer; the personal security keys for these wallets are kept alone on the computer in question. Your security key's online exposure will be reduced as a result of this. However, desktop wallets are still susceptible to hacking if the computer on which they are stored has been infected with malware that is intended to extract private keys and steal bitcoin.

Hardware Wallet A hardware wallet is far more secure than a traditional desktop wallet. The e-wallet refers to any piece of hardware, such as an external device such as a USB drive, that you are able to carry on your person. You are able to transact in complete privacy while using a hardware wallet, which is a further advantage of using one. Because there is no personally identifiable information linked to the hardware, there is no identifying data that may possibly be compromised. Hardware wallets are resistant to virus, and if you lose the wallet, you will be able to retrieve your funds by using a seed phrase even if you lose the wallet itself.

Wallet made of paper

Although it requires a somewhat more advanced knowledge of how digital currencies function, storing Bitcoin in a paper wallet is also a relatively safe way to do so. However, this method does need more time and effort. Produce a paper wallet with an online generator by using any number of dedicated You may webte your wallet, or you can generate it offline for an even higher level of protection. Paper wallets are easy to store since they don't take up a lot of space, and they also provide complete anonymity because all that's on them is a Bitcoin address written in some fashion on a piece of paper. This makes paper wallets ideal for anyone who want to keep their Bitcoin transactions private.

## Where Should One Begin?

First, you need get some Bitcoin.

There are some exchanges that will let you buy certain cryptocurrencies for US Dollars, but it is a better idea to buy Bitcoin first. There are some exchanges that will let you buy particular cryptocurrencies for US Dollars. On any cryptocurrency exchange, you may trade into and out of any other cryptocurrency that is currently on the market if you have some Bitcoin. Keep in mind that it is not necessary for you to purchase a whole Bitcoin.You may purchase Bitcoin using a fractional unit called a Satoshi; for instance, 500 thousand Satoshis is equivalent to 0.005 Bitcoin. You may also go to an exchange that has a USD-BTC pairing in order to try to trade USD for Bitcoin at a lower rate. Coinbase.com is the safest and most popular site to acquire Bitcoin, but you can also try going to an exchange that has a USD-BTC coupling.

It is time to choose an exchange now that you have some Bitcoin in your possession.

Bittrex.com stands out as the most reliable exchange that I've come across. There are other exchanges; some of them are good, some of them are awful, and some of them have already been closed down due to scandals like the one involving Mt. Gox. The news that an exchange has been closed down or that coins have been stolen may cause some people to lose interest in cryptocurrencies completely; nevertheless, I see all of this as a rite of passage for any new market that is still in its infancy.

Rapidly spread over the world of cryptocurrencies.

If you pay attention to the news on Twitter, you will often see smoke before there is a fire. This is the case as long as you remain vigilant. Twitter conversations often revolve on cryptocurrency markets and businesses. Check in on Twitter and other crypto-related forums every day, and be sure to follow any relevant hash tags. Information is power, news is power, and rumors are opportunities.

Trading may begin as soon as Bitcoin has been successfully sent into your exchange account.

However, before you simply choose any cryptocurrencies at random and monitor the charts for them, I strongly advise you to conduct some study beforehand; otherwise, you will be trading without any real knowledge. The easiest way to get familiar with each coin is to do research on it, such as "Cannabaccoann" (where "ann" stands for "an announcement"). This search phrase will take you to the forum at bitcointalk.org, where you can see the official announcement thread for Cannabcoin.

Important information, such as a coin's total supply, technical specifics, development goals, mission statement, and community speculation, may be found in the coin's official announcement thread. In addition, Twitter is an excellent resource for not just keeping up with the latest news, but also locating web sites and other forums. associated with a cryptocurrency.

The most fundamental but significant aspect to keep in mind is as follows:

Buy cheap and sell high is the goal. After it has been dumped on the market is the best moment to purchase a coin.

Why? Because individuals who did not cash out during the pump and are hence referred to as "bag holders" do not want to sell their coin at the bottom, when it would be sold at a much lower price. It should go without saying that if the price of a currency that you have purchased is moving upward quickly, you should liquidate your holdings and convert them into Bitcoin as soon as possible. And if it is a good company that you want to invest in for the long term, you should be sure to buy back in after a dump if the price drops. It is often more beneficial to concentrate on acquiring excellent coins rather than making more Bitcoin, since the value of a good currency will almost always increase in the future.

When you are just starting to get your feet wet with cryptocurrencies, all of the technical language might seem like it is too much to handle. It is essential to acquire knowledge, yet as of right now, If you are just somewhat interested in trading and investing, all you need to have an advantage over other traders is a common-sense grasp of business, consumer demand, and economics.

a synopsis of the procedures

1 The first thing you should do is go out and get yourself some Bitcoin. There is no need to buy a whole Bitcoin at this time. You may get started by buying Bitcoin fractions, which are more often referred to as Satoshis. It is generally agreed that Coinbase.com is the most reliable and well-liked platform on which to purchase bitcoins.

2 After you have acquired some Bitcoin, the next step is to locate an exchange where you may sell or buy it. There are a lot of trustworthy exchanges out there, so if you have any questions or would want to utilize our services, please do not hesitate to contact our brokers. It is heartening to learn that the majority of people in the Bitcoin and cryptocurrency world are familiar with which exchanges and market places can be trusted the most. 3 After you have deposited enough Bitcoins into your account, you will be able to begin trading. However, doing some research before trading is preferable than doing it without any preparation at all. The official threads

relating to the announcement of a currency include a number of crucial pieces of information, including the mission statement of the coin, the technical characteristics of the coin, the total supply of coins, community speculation, and a great deal more. Twitter is also an important resource for information about cryptocurrencies.

4 Finding out the appropriate information at the appropriate time and having an understanding of how it interacts with the market will make it much simpler for you to predict how the market will behave in the future. For someone who trades in cryptocurrencies, technical analysis is also quite important.

5 The most important thing for you to take away from this lesson is to always remember to "buy low and sell high."

6 When purchasing coins, it is important to carefully choose the time. After the

coin has been dumped into circulation is the best time to make a purchase.

## Which Nfts Now Hold The Record For The Highest Price Tag?

I won't include the top 10 most expensive NFTs to date since the list is always being updated, but I will list some of the most remarkable NFTs based on their price, rarity, and uniqueness.

The First 5,000 Days of BeepleWith Each and Every Day

This particular piece of NFT art was sold at Christie's for the astounding figure of $69 million, which is, to this day, the most anybody has ever paid for an NFT and is also the most expensive piece of art created by a living artist. It is comprised of five hundred works of art, all of which were produced in May of 2007.

The piece of artwork was acquired by VigneshSundaresan, popularly known as MetaKovan, who subsequently exhibited it at a digital art museum located inside the Metaverse, which is a shared virtual world.

Stay Free is an album by Edward Snowden that was released in 2021.

This work of art displays a picture of Edward Snowden superimposed above court papers demonstrating that the National Security Agency in the United States unlawfully collects and aggregates data on a large number of people. That was a work of art that had been donated to a charitable organization known as the Freedom of the Press Foundation, and it had been auctioned for more than $5.4 million.

Crazy Dog Jones when use the Replicator

Because of this particular work of art, this artist is presently the live Canadian artist who commands the highest price per sale. It is also one of a kind due to the fact that it will produce fresh NFTs every 28 days, each of which will have a value for resale. The buyer, who may end up with ownership of up to 220 distinct NFTs that they may resell, will see a healthy return on their investment thanks to this opportunity. If you can get so much more out of it, then the price tag of $4.1 million is absolutely justified.

Quantum has been assigned to Kevin McCoy.

This particular NFT is one of a kind in the sense that it was the very first of its kind ever established in 2014. Using technology that he developed in collaboration with the programmer Anil Dash, the artist issued the token on Namecoin in May of 2014. They attempted to explain it to those in attendance at the New Museum in New York City, but all they got was laughter.

On the other hand, as the old saying goes, "Who's laughing now?" I think it's safe to say that with 1.4 million dollars under their belts, the two designers are smiling all the way to the bank.

Carry the Switch in your Pak.

The owner of the piece of art has the option of switching the picture on the painting to something completely different. The digital realm is opening up new possibilities for artists in terms of how they express their work. On the other hand, once the new owner chooses to flip the switch, there is no way to reverse the decision.

It was part of a collection of seven digital art works that was sold at Sotheby's for $17 million, so it is easy for me to see why the owner would be reluctant to make any changes to the item.

Gunky's Uprising counts as a 3LAU.

This project honors the disc jockey (DJ) and electronic musician by combining animated artwork with a music video to commemorate the third anniversary of the release of his album Ultraviolet. It is not surprising that he is offering a couple of further works of art for sale for a price of $1.3 million.

These unreleased recordings have music, and when they are bought, the customer has the choice of naming the tracks.

The Devil Himself With the assistance of Destination Hexagonia

This full-length performance that lasts for one hour was made by the Dutch DJ, record producer, musician, and composer who is recognized for his work in electronic music.

The proprietor was given a hard drive in the style of a science fiction story that contained the unique copy of the file. Because of this, it is considered a rare collectable and is estimated to be worth around $1.2 million.

Don Diablo is now working on comic books for the NFT.

## The Market ForCryptocurrencies

Trading in virtual currencies: what exactly is that?

Trading cryptocurrencies is quite similar to trading shares in that participants guess on the direction that cryptocurrency prices will go. For this purpose, a trading platform known as Contracts for Difference (CFD) is used. The Contract for Difference (CFD) gives you the opportunity to bet on price increases and decreases across a wide range of worldwide marketplaces, including those of cryptocurrencies. You are free to examine whatever cryptocurrency you choose without ever having to worry about actually owning any of those currencies. By doing so, you will be able to carefully choose the actions that come after this one. If you believe that the value of a cryptocurrency is going to increase, you may "go long" by purchasing the cryptocurrency. On the other hand, if you believe that the value of the cryptocurrency is likely to decrease, you can "go short" by selling your coin.

However, in order to have access to all of the information about these underlying markets, you will first need to obtain full exposure and then make a deposit, which is also referred to as margin. Your profit and loss are normally calculated based on your position; however, you may amplify either one by leveraging your assets or by paying a margin. Both of these strategies include paying a fee.

You may also trade cryptocurrencies with one another via a marketplace known as an exchange. You will have to go through your own learning curve in order to get the most of the knowledge that this provides. Before you are able to sell your currency on an exchange, you will first need to ensure that you have an exchange account, add the value of your assets, and keep your money in a wallet. To make a purchase via an exchange, you will need to first acquire the physical coins for your own collection.

142

How exactly do the marketplaces for cryptocurrencies function?

Because cryptocurrency is a decentralized type of money, the market for cryptocurrencies is similarly decentralized, as is already common knowledge. This indicates that there is neither a centralized authority nor a formal organization, such as a bank or the government, that is monitoring or influencing the flow of the market. The market is dependent on the internet and computers, which are the primary factors that have contributed to its evolution into a worldwide market. The market can be watched to some degree thanks to the exchanges, which enable the purchase and sale of cryptocurrencies as well as their storage in wallets. In other words, the exchanges make it possible to buy and sell cryptocurrencies.

Because cryptocurrency is not like the real currencies that we use in our day-to-day transactions, its movements have to be documented in order for it to exist digitally. This is because of the difference in nature between the two. Because of this, we have something called blockchain, which is similar to a book ledger in that it keeps a record of all the transactions involving cryptocurrencies and operates as if it were a book ledger. Whenever I wish to sell part of my bitcoin to another person, I use my cryptocurrency wallet to complete the transaction. On the other hand, until that transaction has been validated and published to the blockchain, it will not be considered complete. In order to add a transaction to the blockchain, it first has to be mined by crypto miners. Crypto miners are the ones who are in charge of validating and recording the transaction, and if they mine it successfully, they may get a reward in the form of bitcoin.

When it comes to trading cryptocurrencies, what are some of the best kept secrets?

Trading cryptocurrencies demands a lot of courage, patience, and resiliency since the process can be quite stressful and your valuable assets are on the line. Being a trader of cryptocurrencies requires you to have these traits. However, as a trader, there are actions that you can do to guarantee that you are always performing at the highest level possible. Here are some straightforward and actionable trading tips from experienced cryptocurrency investors:

1. Always be ready.

The key to your success in crypto is having a well-defined strategy and being well-prepared for it. You need to establish a standard for yourself for how you will behave in the event that the market moves in certain ways. Once you have made that decision, you need to ensure that you stick to this strategy absolutely no matter what happens. If you want to be successful, you need to make sure that you are ready for everything that might happen, and you should also have a backup strategy in place in case things don't go as planned.

145

2. Examine each of your coins.

Keep in mind that the market for cryptocurrencies is now in a bear market. It is going through a difficult time right now, but it will eventually come out on the other side of this. As a result, you should ensure that your coins are consolidated. Sort out the coins that will retain their worth over time from the ones that won't, and then slice them up proportionately.

3. Don't pay attention to those who doubt you.

Skeptics have a lot of power and influence since there is a lot of bad discussion around cryptocurrencies and its future. As a result, it is simple to be swayed and impacted by them. Remember that the most essential thing to keep in mind is to ignore this unfavorable noise and to not let it to influence your trading selections. There will never be a day when there are no pessimists, but that does not mean you should abandon the things you have faith in.

4. Locate your other players.

If you do it with the proper people, trading cryptocurrencies can be a lot of fun. All you need is a supportive community. Get in contact with some of your other pals who are just as obsessed with trading cryptocurrencies as you are, and exchange information with them. You could even wish to build relationships with people all around the world by participating in cryptocurrency forums, which are places where you can read about genuine bitcoin news and trends.

5. Make use of financial instruments.

You can engage in trading these days thanks to the abundance of tools that are easily accessible and provide you with the ability to do in-depth research and analysis of the market. Don't be hesitant to put these skills to work for you; you can only benefit. Trading View pro,

Hacked.com, and signalgroups.com are examples of well-known trading tools.

## Where Can I Use My Tokens Or Coins To Make A Purchase?

Finding out which businesses and service providers accept transactions in non-fiat currencies and which do not may be a time-consuming and difficult process. These platforms and search engines may be useful to you if your primary objective is to make purchases using cryptocurrencies rather than to make investments in the cryptocurrency market.

1. Open Market Bazaar

This is an open-source initiative that makes it easier for people to engage in e-commerce in a market that is completely decentralized. A group of software engineers led by Amir Taaki conceived of the idea to construct a decentralized online marketplace in the beginning stages of the project. However, since Taaki did not intend to extend the project, a different developer by the name of Brian Hoffman took ownership of it and developed it further. To be honest with Hoffman, he later rewrote the core programming that controlled the first project so that none of Taaki's work was used in his enterprise.

Now, what exactly are the capabilities of OpenBazaar? You may think of it as a knockoff of Amazon that genuinely helps you save money on your purchases. Because it utilizes the technology behind digital money, you will be able to make purchases without being required to pay any extra costs. At this exact moment, Bitcoin and every other cryptocurrency adhere to one of its fundamental principles.

2. Spend some money

Spendabit is an extension of the idea behind OpenBazaar that goes a little bit farther. It claims that it is the first Bitcoin product search engine ever created anywhere in the globe. You may have access to a number of different e-commerce websites at the same time, which means that instead of looking for the item you want to buy on a single platform, you would be able to search across numerous platforms at the same time. They collect products from a wide variety of retailers, such as Fancy.com, Overstock.com, and Newegg, all of which accept Bitcoin as a payment option. Spendabit is a platform that allows customers to browse and buy the wares offered by a large number of freshly emerged and more modestly sized retailers. 3.Purse.io

Are you looking for something with a somewhat different mode of operation? After that, go to the Purse.io website. The purpose of this platform is to facilitate the pairing of gift card owners with customers who own Bitcoin. If you are interested in purchasing an item and someone happens to have a gift card for that item, then they may buy that thing for you in exchange for some bitcoins if you are interested in making the purchase. People often refer to situations like these as "win-win."

4. Coinaphere

There's a good probability that all you want to know is the most recent information on which businesses and retailers currently accept Bitcoin. Coinmap is likely to become one of your go-to apps if you're looking for a straightforward approach to accomplish that goal. It features a UI that is rather easy to use and is nice to users. You will have access to a digital version of a globe map that pinpoints the locations of establishments that are willing to take the contents of your digital wallet as payment.

5. The Coin ATM Radar

CoinATMRadar is there to save the day for you if you ever find yourself in a sticky scenario where the only cash you have is in the form of bitcoins and no other currency. This tool will help you zero in on Bitcoin ATMs, which are machines that change digital currency, such as bitcoins, into fiat currency, such as dollars. However, it will not link you with businesses who support Bitcoin.

All of these new resources, including the most recent one, have a single goal in common, and that is to make digital currencies, beginning with Bitcoin, accessible to the general public. They also want to bring to the attention of those who are already making use of Bitcoin the fact that there is a lot more they can do with it than simply invest in it. This is achieved through creating ad establishing platforms and other services similar to the five that were discussed earlier in this paragraph.

Cryptocurrency's Many Advantages

There are a number of appealing advantages that come along with cryptocurrency. A portion of this may be attributed to the blockchain technology that was discussed before. Transactions and controls are carried out in an encrypted format while being continuously watched.

• Brief Overview of the History of Money

Since the beginning of time, people have looked to everything that is in short supply as a source of value. In the beginning, people engaged in trade in order to convert one thing for another. But how can you possibly buy a cow if you only have two chickens? They needed a third component, so they chose the most unique seashells they could find. Then there were coins made out of precious metals. At initially, the worth of coins was determined not by the imprint that was placed on them but by their weight. After some time had passed, the true value of the coin was finally imprinted upon it.

The next step was the introduction of paper money that was backed by precious metals such as gold. The idea was that you could go into a bank and ask for the gold value of your banknotes at any time. After that, the paper was uncoupled from the Gold Standard and became unbacked, which made it possible for money creation to thrive. At the moment, this is what we mean when we talk about 'fiat' money.

The problem is that there is an abundance of fiat money. The value of money decreases each year as a result of the possibility that more of it will be produced. Gold is the only form of wealth storage that does not lose its value over time. On the other hand, gold is difficult to store, split, or transport about.

In order to provide a comprehensive account of the span of time covered by the History of Money, it is necessary to discuss the scarcity of cryptocurrencies. Consider the most popular one, Bitcoin, for instance. As was said before, there will never be more than 21 million manufactured, which suggests that limited availability is built into the system.

• There is no participation from a third party

When using conventional means of finance, such as when buying a new house, beginning a new company, or investing in a new vehicle, there is always a process that must be adhered to. Engaging the services of a third party is required in some capacity or another in order to complete the procedure. We are discussing attorneys, owners, as well as other external factors such as delays, documentation, extra expenditures, and so on. Because of this, a significant amount of time, money, and effort will be wasted, and as a result, some individuals will quit up. A recent financial obligation of mine required that I transfer money to the United States. In order to complete this task, I needed to contact my bank. To start the procedure, I had to wait in line for more than eight minutes while listening to music. I was quite annoyed. After that, I was billed for the cost of delivering the money as well as an exorbitant Foreign Exchange rate that did not match to the actual rate.

Last but not least, due to the fact that the transaction was processed via an intermediary bank, I was informed that they would very likely charge me, even though they were unable to specify the amount of the fee. I was told that it would take between three and five business days for the money to arrive. Due to the fact that it was such a large amount of money, the whole transaction most likely set me back more than $200, if not even more when you take into account the Foreign Exchange spread. I really didn't have a lot of other choices, so I had no choice but to say yes to everything.

When I use cryptos, I can send bitcoins immediately from my computer to theirs via the internet in less than ten minutes. There is not only no spread, but also no cost for foreign currency exchange (Forex), and there are no middlemen involved. And the whole thing may not set me back more than ten dollars.

If you want to make significant time and financial savings, investing in cryptocurrencies is the way to go. To put it another way, when you utilize cryptocurrencies, you are in complete control of your own financial situation. A "decentralized" system is what's meant to be described here. It is possible to send and receive money throughout the world at any time and from any location at any given moment. Your transactions are protected from practically all forms of government intervention, and the processing costs are kept to an absolute minimum, which frees users from the obligation of paying extra fees to banks or other types of financial organizations.

Imagine this happening in every part of life, from the signing of formal contracts between organizations to the transport of money throughout the globe; from the placing of funds in escrow when buying a property to the making of payments online. Any place where there is a person acting as a "middleman," who is either

1. Bringing the pace of the procedure down

2. Putting an increase in the price.

• Traditional currencies are subject to a greater level of risk.

The vast majority of individuals in today's society carry about very little cash at any one time. Customers may, as an alternative, pay for their purchases using a variety of credit cards, debit cards, and other payment cards that are accepted in their nation. There is nothing inherently wrong with it; but, if the business loses its connection to the server or their machine breaks down and you do not have any cash on you, you will not be able to pay for the item. When you use your card, you are effectively granting the end-recipient access to your whole credit limit. Even if the transaction is very little, the fact that you are providing someone else your card in order for them to access your account constitutes a "breach" of some kind.

A significant portion of this "breach" is now considered to be safe to use as a result of the implementation of several security precautions, such as "PIN-enabled" or other methods. After then, the shop will start the process of collecting payment by 'drawing' the agreed-upon sum from your account using the information included on your card. That is not how virtual currencies function in any way. It does not use a method known as "pull," but rather "pushes" the amount of bitcoin that must be given to or received from other cryptocurrency holders. This is done without the need for any additional information. It is possible to make payments without linking your data to either you or the transaction itself. You have the option of backing up and encrypting your account in order to increase the level of protection afforded to the security of your cash.

The network's security for Bitcoin, Ether, and other popular cryptocurrencies is improved when individuals are given the ability to control the regulation of their own transactions.

• Protection from Financial Fraud

We commonly hear about instances in which one person's credit card is used by another individual without the approval of the card's owner. When he calls the number listed on the back of his card, he learns that his card has been used in transactions for which he did not provide authorization. This is what the legal system calls a fraud case. Because it might be difficult to determine who committed the fraud in the first place, the fraudsters who committed these crimes almost always get away with their deception. Additionally, getting the attention of law enforcement in order to launch an investigation is a far more difficult task.

Fraud cannot be committed using bitcoin because of its decentralized nature. Because your personal information is shielded from prying eyes in this way, you won't have to worry about having your identity stolen. Keep in mind that bitcoin is a kind of digital money that is constructed via the use of code. Because each cryptocurrency is held in digital form, it is impossible for senders to create counterfeit versions of it. There is no transmission of personally identifiable information since the transactions cannot be undone.

This keeps the security intact and shields businesses from any possible damages that may be incurred as a result of fraudulent situations. It is difficult to commit fraud with these cryptocurrencies because of their decentralized nature and the blockchain technology that is already in place.

It is impossible for anybody or any organization to make changes to it since it is cryptographically secure. Every computer has a copy of every transaction, and they are in continual communication with one another so that they may share this information. Because there is no way for someone to get in and make changes, this is the most secure technique.

If someone tried to hack into the Blockchain, they would be wasting their time if they just broke into one or a few machines since the information on the majority of computers would always win in the end. In order to make a modification, they would need to break into 51% of the computers that are part of the Blockchain all around the globe. It is impossible to get the necessary level of computer power.

Additionally, some time would be required. Since the data on the blockchain is updated or refreshed every few minutes, a potential hacker has a few minutes to get in before everything is wiped clean and the process starts over again.

After then, they would have to begin everything from the very beginning again. In addition to the fact that they would have just a few minutes to get into 51% of the hundreds of devices that make up the Blockchain all around the globe, they would also have to hack into those machines.

• A sense of universality

Throughout the course of history, countries from all over the globe have used a wide array of methods of monetary exchange. We had methods of trading goods for money as well as exchanging money for goods.

When merchants traveled to other nations, it was only then that they learned how to trade successfully with one another. As a result of these discoveries and improvements, people all over the globe today have access to a variety of different methods to buy and sell currency. Nevertheless, despite all of the improvements, we are still unable to complete foreign transactions without encountering problems. Always on the table are worries about currency, bank authorizations, incorrect payment methods, and a variety of other problems that company owners and people traveling internationally encounter. The fact of the matter is that different nations do not all operate their financial systems in the same way. It is possible that other countries may not accept your card or money, which can be a significant obstacle for certain individuals. For example, extra processing fees are applied by the majority of online banking, payment, and currency exchange systems.

On the other hand, the value of cryptocurrencies does not depend on the currency exchange rates, transaction fees, interest rates, or any other associated costs of any nation. They may be used without incident at any time or place in any part of the globe, and there are no restrictions on where or when they can be used. In addition, it helps you save a lot of time and money by reducing the amount of money you have to spend on international money transfers. As a consequence of this, Bitcoin operates on a global platform, which makes transactions more practical than the conventional method of transferring money from one bank to another.